In this lively devotional, Spence does an incredible job of bringing the words of Jesus to life in the very soul of the reader. Get ready as she leads you on a fishing expedition to deal with the depths of who you are and who you are becoming. Don't be afraid to expose the anxiety holding you back from attaining all Christ wants for your life. You will finish refreshed, renewed, and thankful for the brilliance the author uses to gracefully walk you past life's biggest fears. We don't like to deal with us, but in 31 days, you will be glad you did.

—Scott Obenchain, Lead Pastor
Blue Ridge Church, Christiansburg, VA

In Donette Spence's new book, *Seeds of Success,* you will be given practical, life-changing principals to break down negative belief patterns. Jesus never intended us to remain complacent and stuck in life. Fear is not part of the child of God's demeanor. Fear immobilizes and causes us to stagnate and dissipate in our faith. *Seeds of Success* is written so that you will develop a habit of success. I challenge you to put these seeds of success into your life and see what Jesus can do with and through you.

—Dr. Nick Gough, MTS, D.Min.
Author of *When The Old Becomes New*
Senior Pastor, Hope Chapel, Apex, NC

In Donette's book, *Seeds of Success,* she leads you from the shallow waters with God and teaches you how to explore the deeper depths with Him. She is raw but humorous in her approach. She has a true desire to see people go deeper because that's where the true success stems from. Donette has the ability to get you off the couch and into your purpose by looking and assessing what truly matters. *You will enjoy her real and down to earth style.* If you want to go deeper, *Seeds of Success* will help get you there.

—Dr. Lauren Clark, Evangelist, Missionary,
President of Here Am I Ministries, Haiti Representative for
HAPN and GAPN,
Missionary Director for REIF

Are you searching for ways to overcome those things that have hindered you from living your life at its fullest potential? Well, this is the book for you! You will enjoy the insightful and life-changing wisdom Donette presents in a most relevant and down to earth style. Whether you've been crippled by past failures or anxious over the unknown possibilities of success, Seeds of Success will renew your hope and provide practical steps to becoming that person you know you were destined to be!

—Sharon R. Atkinson, Administrative Pastor
New Life Christian Ministries, Roanoke, VA

Seeds of Success

Seeds of Success

31 Days to Blow the Fear of Success out of the Water

Donette W. Spence

SEEDS OF SUCCESS Copyright © 2020 by Donette W. Spence
All rights reserved.

Printed in the United States of America
Published by Author Academy Elite
PO Box 43, Powell, OH 43065
www.AuthorAcademyElite.com

All rights reserved. This book contains material protected under International and Federal Copyright Laws and Treaties. Any unauthorized reprint or use of this material is prohibited. No part of this book may be reproduced or transmitted in any form or by any means, electronic or mechanical, including photocopying, recording, or by any information storage and retrieval system, without express written permission from the author.

Identifiers:

Library of Congress Control Number: 2020916021
978-1-64746-459-2 (Paperback)
978-1-64746-460-8 (Hardback)
978-1-64746-461-5 (ebook)

Available in paperback, hardback, e-book, and audiobook

Scripture quotations marked TPT are from The Passion Translation®. Copyright © 2017, 2018 by Passion & Fire Ministries, Inc. Used by permission. All rights reserved. ThePassionTranslation.com. Scriptures marked (KJV) are taken from the King James Version. Scriptures marked NKJV are taken from the New King James Version (NKJV): Copyright© 1982 by Thomas Nelson, Inc. Used by permission. All rights reserved. Scriptures marked (NIV) are taken from the New International Version, NIV, Copyright© 1973, 1978, 1984, 2011 by Biblica, Inc.™. Used by permission of Zondervan. All rights reserved worldwide. Scriptures marked CEV are taken from the Contemporary English Version (CEV): Scripture taken from the Contemporary English Version copyright© 1995 by the American Bible Society. Used by permission. Scriptures marked (ESV) are from the ESV® Bible (The Holy Bible, English Standard Version®), copyright © 2001 by Crossway, a publishing ministry of Good News Publishers. Used by permission. All rights reserved." Scripture quotations marked MSG are taken from *THE MESSAGE*, copyright © 1993, 2002, 2018 by Eugene H. Peterson. Used by permission of NavPress. All rights reserved. Represented by Tyndale House Publishers, a Division of Tyndale House Ministries.

Any Internet addresses (websites, blogs, etc.) and telephone numbers printed in this book are offered as a resource. They are not intended in any way to be or imply an endorsement by Author Academy Elite, nor does Author Academy Elite vouch for the content of these sites and numbers for the life of this book.

Dedication

This book is dedicated to my family: *Lots of Crazy, Lots of Loud & Bunches of Love*, describes them perfectly!

To the *Love of My Life*, husband and *soul mate* of 34 years, Randy. He is always a source of incredible positivity, reminding me that I can do it. Always believing in me and embracing my weird ways, he pushes me to obtain every ambition that God put inside of me. He read the manuscript *many* times, 31 days was multiplied greatly for him. He has and continues to make life and love fun!

To our daughters, Kristen (Special K) and Brittany (Britz). The hours you simply listened and encouraged, always believing in me as your Mom and even greater, your friend. There is nothing like the friendship of a Daughter. Through much laughter, we continue to learn how to do life together.

To our Son-in-Law, Maxwell. Thanks for listening on the beach many times, to my dreams about writing, even when I couldn't articulate what the book was really about. Cheers to your honesty and simply loving me for me.

To our precious and fun grandkids, Baxter & Eliza. From *Dragonfly moments* with Baxter to *Deep Eye moments* with Eliza, you make life incredibly fun. May you obtain success every day of your life.

Table of Contents

What Is Success to You? 17
S1 Undivided Attention 19
S2 Multi or Switch? 21
S3 The Direct Order 23
S4 Jesus, the Fish Whisperer 27
S5 The Promise 29
S6 Mystery of the Deep 33
S7 Night Shift 35
S8 Because You Say So 37
S9 Let 41
S10 Success 45
S11 Come Here Fishy, Fishy, Fishy 47
S12 Profit 49
S13 Who's Gonna Help You? 53
S14 J LOL 55
S15 Aahhh, the Aroma 59
S16 Balance the Fish 61
S17 Rhythm's Relation to Balance 63

S18	Oh Snap, Jesus!	67
S19	Self-Sabotage	71
S20	Jesus the Space Invader	75
S21	Unworthy	79
S22	Ignored from the Throne Room	81
S23	Comfort = Failure	83
S24	Next Level	87
S25	Awestruck	89
S26	Fear Stinks	93
S27	From Now On	97
S28	Intimate Vulnerability Vessel	99
S29	Opening & Closing Seasons	103
S30	The Complexity of Success	107
S31	Wildest Imagination Exceeded	109
One Last Deep Drench Dive		111

Foreword

I have known Pastor Donette Spence and her husband, Randy, for over 20 years. Donette has always been a fearless pacesetter. No matter the task, she would pursue it with confidence that the Lord Jesus would help her accomplish it. I am proud to say she is a spiritual daughter in the faith. She has been a major part in our ministry and life through the years. I am not surprised that the Holy Spirit would use her to pen this book, *Seeds of Success*. She has lived this out in her everyday life as a fearless leader, never giving up, no matter the odds. As you read this book, you will be inspired and motivated to pursue your God-given dreams. As you Dip, Dive, and Drench yourself in the word of the Lord, you will overcome against all the odds.

—Dr. Eddie R. Mitchell
Senior Pastor, RiversEdge Church
President, RiversEdge International Fellowship

Preface

Welcome to Book 1 of the SOS series.
The *Satiate Our Souls* series is designed to introduce and/or deepen your relationship with Jesus.

SOS: Morse code sequence of three dots, three dashes, three dots: …---…
SOS: Internationally recognized symbol for distress or help
SOS: Instantly recognized with its symmetry:
Palindrome (a word that reads the same backwards and forwards)
Ambigram (a word that looks identical upside-down or right-side up)
When carved into a snowbank or spelled out on a beach, SOS is SOS
So, regardless of the way a rescue chopper approaches, SOS is seen

Satiate: To satisfy fully or to excess

SOS: Satiate Our Souls is the cry of many hearts that are tired and weary as life sucks the water from our lives. Allow this series to show you how to keep your soul satiated with the living water of Jesus. Be fully satisfied and beyond … to excess!
SOS: Send an SOS to Jesus, regardless of where you are or what's happening, He will see your SOS and satiate your soul! Be Satiated!

If you don't know Jesus, here's the simple prayer:
Jesus, I believe you died on the cross and rose again for me. I ask for forgiveness of my sins and invite you to live life with me. Be the Lord of my life. Amen.
If you prayed this prayer, contact me so I can celebrate with you: realandraw.withdonette@gmail.com

Fear of Failure:

Scared of *not* reaching your goal.

Uncommonly known as

Atychiphobia

Fear of Success:

Scared that

you *will* reach your goal and the unknown hits you smack upside the face!

Uncommonly known as

Achievemephobia

OUCH!

It's easy to admit when you fear failure. On the flip side, we're usually unwilling to accept we're scared to succeed. Fear of success is rampant, often disguised with the mask of the fear of failure.

If you fail, you go back to something you know. When you succeed, it's something new and uncharted territory, which can be so scary. When you find the courage to say no to that fear, you'll leap into success, experience purpose, and collide with passion, which equals joy!

So, I'm giving you seeds so that you'll experience a new level of success in your life when you use them. It's going to take hard, reflective work. You'll sift and even dig through to your core and make peace with areas of your inner being you may not have been aware of. But the results are so worth it. Give all of you, and make a commitment to finish, and get it done!

Dive into the depths and drench yourself in Jesus.

Success is waiting for you …

What Is Success to You?

Success is different for every person. Success can mean:

- Getting out of bed
- Running a race
- Finishing the race
- Winning the race
- Making it another day in your marriage
- Receiving a new position to further your career
- Starting a business
- Receiving a raise
- Winning a person to Jesus
- Losing Weight
- Exercising
- Finishing a work out
- Catching a fish
- Eating the fish
- Teaching someone how to fish
- A continuous journey

What success will you activate with this book?

When you are successful, your life will change! What scares you about that?

Seeds of Success Is Birthed from This True Story ...

Luke 5:1–11 (TPT)

On one occasion, Jesus was preaching to the crowds on the shore of Lake Galilee. There was a vast multitude of people pushing to get close to Jesus to hear the word of God. He noticed two fishing boats at the water's edge, with the fishermen nearby, rinsing their nets. Jesus climbed into the boat belonging to Simon Peter and asked him, "Let me use your boat. Push it off a short distance away from the shore so I can speak to the crowds." Jesus sat down and taught the people from the boat. When he had finished, he said to Peter, "Now row out to deep water to cast your nets and you will have a great catch." "Master," Peter replied, "we've just come back from fishing all night and didn't catch a thing. But if you insist, we'll go out again and let down our nets because of your word." When they pulled up their nets, they were shocked to see a huge catch of fish, so much that their nets were ready to burst! They waved to their business partners in the other boat for help. They ended up completely filling both boats with fish until their boats began to sink! When Simon Peter saw this astonishing miracle, he knelt at Jesus' feet and begged him, "Go away from me, Master, for I am a sinful man!" Simon Peter and the other fishermen—including his fishing partners, Jacob[c] and John, the sons of Zebedee—were awestruck over the miracle catch of fish. Jesus answered, "Do not yield to your fear, Simon Peter. From now on you will catch men for salvation!" After pulling their boats to the shore, they left everything behind and followed Jesus.

We will use these 11 verses over the next 31 days to dive in, and we'll use some more than once. Okay, get ready. You're about to launch onto the boat with Jesus and head out to the deep. Success, here we come!

A true friend is one who overlooks your failures
and tolerates your success!
—Doug Larson

S1
Undivided Attention

Luke 5:1–3 (TPT)

On one occasion, Jesus was preaching to the crowds on the shore of Lake Galilee. There was a vast multitude of people pushing to get close to Jesus to hear the word of God. He noticed two fishing boats at the water's edge, with the fishermen nearby, rinsing their nets. Jesus climbed into the boat belonging to Simon Peter and asked him, "Let me use your boat. Push it off a short distance away from the shore so I can speak to the crowds."
(Of note: Lake Galilee is also known as the "Sea of Galilee" and "Lake of Gennesaret")

Jesus needed a place to preach; He didn't need a fancy podium. He wanted a place away from the people so they'd stop crowding Him, and He could breathe. (I know you've had that happen … just sayin'). Jesus looked around and saw two boats available. Peter's boat was one of the two. Jesus only needed one, which meant it was a 50/50 chance to choose Peter's boat. But yep, you guessed it! He chooses Peter's boat, hopped in, and said to Peter, "Push it off a short distance away from the shore so I can speak to the crowds." Jesus didn't have a microphone, and yet He wants to be pushed out even farther. Why? Jesus wanted the undivided attention of Peter. And there is a 100% chance that He wants your undivided attention too! So, hop in your boat with Jesus, and push off to a place where He has your undivided attention. Just you and Him. Journal what He says to you about success in your life, now is a perfect time to get it started.

Dip ...
What keeps you from giving your undivided attention to Jesus?

_____
_____
_____

Dive ---
What will you do differently each day to give Jesus your undivided attention? (Yeah, I know, it requires change!)

_____
_____
_____

Drench ...
By the way, there is a 100% chance that Jesus wants to use your boat and get in it with you. The question is, are you willing? If so, what does that look like for you? If you are willing for him to use your boat, do you enjoy being in the boat alone with Jesus?

_____
_____
_____

> The most valuable commodity of the 21st century will be undivided attention.
> —Phil Cooke

Success is waiting for you ...

S2
Multi or Switch?

Luke 5:2 (TPT)

<u>Take 2</u>: *He noticed two fishing boats at the water's edge, with the fishermen nearby, rinsing their nets.*

Peter was washing and hanging his nets and watching Jesus. Is that like reading the Word, scrolling the feed on Facebook, texting a friend, and watching TV at the same time? (Yeah, I've been watching you!) Multi-tasking is a myth.

Okay, so I struggle with multi—I mean—*switch* tasking. Nancy K. Napier, PhD said, "Much recent neuroscience research tells us that the brain doesn't really do tasks simultaneously, as we thought (hoped) it might. In fact, we just switch tasks quickly. Each time we move from hearing music to writing a text or talking to someone, there is a stop/start process that goes on in the brain.[1]

Peter was really switch tasking. He washed and hung a net, then watched Jesus. He or anyone else (yes, even women!) are slower when multi-tasking. So, in this case, Peter was slower doing all those tasks than if he would have stopped, thrown down the nets, and gave his full attention to Jesus. The nets could wait; they were empty anyway, right? Switch-tasking is proven to lower our productivity by 40% (even on the low end, that's huge)! Jory MacKay, said, "On an average day, we normally use 56 apps and websites, jump from one task to another nearly 300 times per day and switch between documents and pages within a site 1,300 times per day.[2]

SEEDS OF SUCCESS

Dip ...
Peter wasn't completely interested in what Jesus said. He did what we all do—we pay attention to Jesus, but at the same time, we switch-task. What is more interesting or preferable to you than Jesus?

_____
_____
_____
_____

Dive ---
The big question is what will you do to stop switch-tasking today when it comes to Jesus? (Neither of us have any time to waste)

I dare you to stop. Try it for 20 minutes right now.

_____
_____
_____
_____

Drench ...
When you weren't switch-tasking, what was different?

_____
_____
_____
_____

Hint:
When you stop switch-tasking, you will enter into a realm of relationship with Jesus you have never known before.

Success is waiting for you ...

S3
The Direct Order

Luke 5:4–5 (TPT)

Jesus sat down and taught the people from the boat. When He had finished, he said to Peter, "Now, row out to deep water to cast your nets and you will have a great catch." "Master," Peter replied, "we've just come back from fishing all night and didn't catch a thing. But if you insist, we'll go out again and let down our nets because of your word."

Whoa, wait just a minute. Did Jesus seriously just tell Peter what to do? He didn't make a request; He gave a direct order. Oh, snap, Jesus!

The direct order has two elements, and we'll explore the first today:

Command: Give an authoritative order.

Jesus didn't say *please*. He didn't say *when you want to*. He didn't say *pray about it*. (Yeah, you've used that excuse how many times?) He said *do it*, which means do it now.

Without question or hesitation, His kingdom operates under authority from our king, Jesus. When He issues a command, we are to hear, listen, and obey—end of story! But we fight that like crazy, don't we? How can we expect the kingdom to operate in our life properly if we don't acknowledge and obey authority? (Hint, it won't operate properly.)

Living in the USA, a democracy, our rights can sometimes hinder us from understanding authority and direct orders. We insist on our rights and don't like being told what to do. We must submit ourselves to our King, knowing He's got the best plan! Now, don't get all theological on me; of course you have free will. He has the aerial view and knows the map of your life.

THE DIRECT ORDER

Dip ...
So, what command is He giving you in this season of your life? (Cough it up!)

_____
_____
_____
_____

Dive ---
Okay, now that you acknowledged the command, are you willing to do it? If yes, how will you move forward?

If no, it's a great idea to spend some time in prayer and see what's holding you back.

_____
_____
_____
_____

Drench ...
When a general in the military gives an order, the answer is *yes, sir* or *yes, ma'am*, regardless of what the soldier's opinion is. Isn't this how we should respond to Jesus? After all, we're in a militant situation; our King has issued commands for us to bring heaven to earth. That, my friend, is militant! Don't let the fact that you have allowed yourself to be commanded mess with your brain. It will actually give you more freedom than you've ever had. I promise!

_____
_____
_____
_____

> I am not afraid of an army of lions led by a sheep;
> I am afraid of an army of sheep led by a lion.
> —Alexander the Great

Success is waiting for you ...

S4

Jesus, the Fish Whisperer

Luke 5:4 (TPT)

<u>Take 2:</u> *Jesus sat down and taught the people from the boat. When he had finished, he said to Peter; "Now row out to deep water to cast your nets and you will have a great catch."*

So, have you ever thought about Jesus talking to the fish and commanding them to jump into Peter's net? ("Now row out to deep water to cast your nets and you will have a great catch"). That's all the fish needed to hear, how to move forward into their destiny, which was part of Peter's destiny. He wanted them to be part of a new move. Have you ever wondered why the fish weren't in the net? Then, they were in the net? I have, and it's nothing short of a miracle.

There's something about His voice. Loving and soft yet commanding with authority and soft like the lamb's *bah*. Yet His voice is authoritative like that of a lion's resounding roar.

Dip ...

Regardless of His voice being loving and soft or commanding with authority, how do you react when you hear His voice? Do you react with belief and forward movement for success or do you take the back seat and wonder if He has the power to bring forth your success? Peter believed the voice of Jesus and allowed the authoritative voice to call forth his destiny, his success, his future.

_____
_____
_____
_____

Dive ---

What is the voice of Jesus saying to you right now about your success? Do you believe Jesus' voice has authority? How will you bypass the fear of success and move forward with what His voice is saying to you?

_____
_____
_____
_____

Drench ...

You need the lion and lamb voice of Jesus in your life. How will you balance the two aspects of Jesus in your life?

_____
_____
_____
_____

He is The Lion and The Lamb and The Great I Am.
-Pinterest.com

Success is waiting for you ...

S5
The Promise

Luke 5:4–5 (TPT)

<u>Take 3:</u> *Jesus sat down and taught the people from the boat. When he had finished, he said to Peter; "Now row out to deep water to cast your nets and you will have a great catch." "Master," Peter replied, "we've just come back from fishing all night and didn't catch a thing. But if you insist, we'll go out again and let down our nets because of your words."*

The second element of the direct order was the promise Jesus gave Peter: "Now row out to deep water to cast your nets and you will have a *great* catch."

Did you catch it? (Pun intended.) Jesus was speaking the promise to Peter that he'd catch fish if he did what he was commanded and was 100% obedient.

There are 1,000s of promises in the Bible:

Philippians 4:19 says, "And m*y God will meet all your needs" (NIV)*

Jeremiah 29:11 says, "*For I know the plans I have for you" (NIV)*

Psalm 37:4 says, *"He will give you the desires of your heart" (NIV)*

Just to name a few.

There are also instances when we venture into the deep with Jesus, and when He makes a promise to you, that promise is all yours! Jesus is amazing like that.

What about the deep part of you still waiting on a promise and wondering when it will happen? What is that promise? Have you obeyed the direct command to receive the promise? If yes, thank Him for the promise coming in the perfect timing (yes, perfect)! If no, ask Him to forgive you for being too stubborn and ask for that second (maybe 32nd) chance. His mercies are new every morning. He'll give you a fresh chance and show you how to work through that.

Habakkuk 2:3 (CEV) says, *At the time I have decided, my words will come true. You can trust what I say about the future. It may take a long time, but keep on waiting-it will happen!*

I want to cut verses like this one out when I'm tired of waiting. But I don't take my scissors out! Instead, I keep trusting and doing my part. Then, bam, it happens! The appointed time is something we neither like or understand. And that's okay. God has a specific time for everything to happen in your life. Remember, He has the aerial view. He sees the end, the beginning, and what we don't even know exists. Write your prayer thanking Him for the wait time to receive the promise.

THE PROMISE

Dip ...
What promise did Jesus give you that you now experience?

_____
_____
_____
_____

Dive ---
Thank Jesus for fulfilling that promise! Take a praise break now (regardless of where you are and who sees you), and thank Him!

_____
_____
_____
_____

Drench ...
Crush dive into the depths. Listen to "Take Courage," featuring Kristene DiMarco. Be patient, and have courage in the waiting.

_____
_____
_____
_____

Success is waiting for you ...

S6

Mystery of the Deep

Luke 5:4 (TPT)

<u>Take 4:</u> *Jesus sat down and taught the people from the boat. When he had finished, he said to Peter, "Now row out to deep water to cast your nets and you will have a great catch."*

The deep is that place of mystery that excites, thrills, and yet scares the beejeebers out of us!

The deep is the place where you can't see the entire picture. Now, you're bored out of your mind and wondering what's next. The deep is the cold, yet captivating, scary, yet sensational, excruciating, yet exhilarating place.

Peter and his friends had cleaned the nets and put them up. Obeying the command of Jesus required taking those clean nets out again, casting them into the water, and then another cleaning when finished. What are your *nets*, and are you willing to cast them yet again?

What do you hope to catch with your clean nets, in the deep?

Psalm 42:7 says, *"Deep calls to deep." (NIV)*

Substance, not surface, meets substance ...

SEEDS OF SUCCESS

Dip ...
What is the deep for you? (Prophetic, miracles, deeper understanding, or something else)

_____
_____
_____
_____

Dive ---
What scares you about the deep, the unknown? What excites you beyond your fear of the unknown?

_____
_____
_____
_____

Drench ...
Take some time and allow the deep of God to meet with the deep of you—it will be amazing! Journal what *the deep* is that you experience with Jesus during this time.

_____
_____
_____
_____

Crush Dive into the Depths ...---...
A sweet song about going deep is "Drink in Deep" by Jake Hamilton. Listen while you go deep! I *double dog dare* you! Journal what else you received as you crush dived into the depths.

Success is waiting for you ...

S7
Night Shift

Luke 5:4–5 (TPT)

Take 5: Jesus sat down and taught the people from the boat. When he had finished, he said to Peter, "Now row out to deep water to cast your nets and you will have a great catch." "Master," Peter replied, "we've just come back from fishing all night and didn't catch a thing. But if you insist, we'll go out again and let down our nets because of your word."

Peter worked the night shift and failed! Fear of failure is huge. It takes courage to be willing to cast your nets again.

People would have asked Peter, *Hey, bro, catch anything last night? Sorry to hear you came up with nothing! Long night, huh? You gonna quit or do it again? Whatcha eating tonight?*

Back in the day, fishing was a huge industry, strenuous, and not always rewarding; it was Peter's source of income. Not only did it hurt his pride, it hurt his wallet!

NO fish = NO money = NO food = NO rent (even for a cheap place to dock his boat)!

SEEDS OF SUCCESS

Dip ...

Right now, name your *night shift* that was or is a failure. Yes, the thing that you throw in Jesus' face when He is talking to you about success. "But Jesus, that thing ..."

_____
_____
_____
_____

Dive ---

Now that you've been straight with Jesus and yourself, forgive Him. Yes, you heard correctly—forgive Jesus. You've been holding that night shift failure over His head. It's not His fault, but many times you place the blame on Him. Write your prayer of forgiveness to Him, and after you've forgiven Him, forgive yourself, and move forward!

_____
_____
_____
_____

Drench ...

What is one step that you will take today to move forward?

_____
_____
_____
_____

Big shout out to all night shifters. The world couldn't operate without y'all! Speaking health, natural rhythms, and sweet sleep time for each of you!

Failure is an event, not a person
—Zig Ziglar

Success is waiting for you ...

S8
Because You Say So

Luke 5:5 (TPT)

<u>Take 6:</u> *"Master," Peter replied, "we've just come back from fishing all night and didn't catch a thing. But if you insist, we'll go out again and let down our nets because of your word."*

Ever said that to Jesus? *Because You say so?* We all have! (Be honest)

Peter was a professional fisherman, an angler, and he knew how to catch fish. Jesus was a carpenter. His expertise was in other areas. He had other gifts and talents, and fishing wasn't on the top of that list. And yet, He gave Peter a YouTube tutorial of how to fish.

Peter, in all humility, accepted the new way to fish, but he let Jesus know he'd fished all night (i.e. I'm tired). We say that to Jesus a lot. Peter also reminds Jesus that they came up with natta, nothing, zero, zippo. We remind Jesus of the failures many times.

Peter's decision, however, is based on something totally different from professional experience and/or education. Peter based it on *"if you say so"* (NLT), *at your word* (ESV).

Do we base our decisions on our status as the professional with experience/education, or do we base these decisions for success on *because you said so?*—especially when we've failed before and maybe feel that we were in His perfect will and still failed. It all comes back to understanding His authority and love for us. Peter gave the words of Jesus the most authority.

Do you trust the words of Jesus, and have you come to that place where you will let down your nets again just because He said so?

Dip ...

Listen to "Everything and Nothing Less" by Chris McClarney, and name that one thing where you have relied upon your personal experience more than the words of Jesus?

_____
_____
_____
_____

Dive ---

What *new way to fish* is Jesus showing you? What is the *if you say so* that Jesus is saying to you?

_____
_____
_____
_____

Drench ...

Will you commit today to trust Him just because He said so? If so, what does that realistically look like in your life? If the answer is no, how can that no be changed to a yes so you can move forward?

_____
_____
_____
_____

Success is waiting for you ...

S9
Let

Luke 5:5 (TPT)

<u>Take 7</u>: *"Master," Peter replied, "we've just come back from fishing all night and didn't catch a thing. But if you insist, we'll go out again and let down our nets because of your word."*

The word *let* has an interesting meaning and usage:
1) To cause, to make
2) To give opportunity to
3) To not prevent or forbid
4) To introduce a request or proposal
5) To express a warning
6) To free from confinement
7) Let is used in verse five: *"I will let down the nets."*
8) Let was also used in verse three: *"Let me use your boat."*
9) Let was also used in Genesis chapter one: *"Let there be."*

Peter said, *"But because you say so, I will let down the nets."* He gave God complete control of his life. Though God is in complete control and can do whatever He wants, whenever, and however He wants, He also gave us free will. Peter allowed his free will to collide with God's perfect will, resulting in an explosion of Holy Spirit creativity. In essence, he said, "Holy Spirit, let us make some fish." When man's spirit is open to God's will by *letting down your net,* it's an express warning: Let him try!

Let is a genesis moment. God brings a freshness to your life, so you need to *let* him. Give Him permission to do whatever, whenever, however He wants.

In Luke 1:38 (ESV), When the angel visited Mary, the mother of Jesus, she responded with *"Let it be to me according to your word."* It would have been hard for teenage virgin Mary to become pregnant by an invisible Holy Spirit. Holy smokes! Yeah, right. Try explaining that one. And she said, *Let it be.* She took the angel at his word to receive Jesus, who *is* the Word! And it changed her life 100%.

Dip ...
What *let* is God asking of you?

_____
_____
_____
_____

Dive ---
The *let* He's asking for could be in an area where you're a virgin. It could be a genesis for something totally new.

_____
_____
_____
_____

Drench ...
It's been a deep day. Listen to "Do What You Want To" by Vertical Worship. Journal what He downloads to you.

_____
_____
_____
_____

Success is waiting for you ...

S10

Success

Luke 5:6 (TPT)

When they pulled up their nets, they were shocked to see a huge catch of fish, so much that their nets were ready to burst!

Finally, success! If you are reading this book, you are experiencing part of my success right now. It feels awesome! What about your success? Your adrenaline would pump, your energy level would overflow, and your words would be uplifting. I mean, who needs caffeine or energy drinks?

SEEDS OF SUCCESS

Dip ...
Simple, what success will you activate in your life through this study? Dream for a minute, and imagine the scene for you. What are your fish?

_____
_____
_____
_____

Dive ---
What does your broken net look like? Be creative, and think big.

_____
_____
_____
_____

Drench ...
I would rather have a broken net that Jesus caused than a perfect net that I controlled. What are you trying to control in your life that is hindering your success and needs to be surrendered to Jesus? Write out a prayer now letting Him know you surrender in that particular area, and allow Him complete control of it. Tell Him you'll be okay with whatever He decides to do with it.

_____
_____
_____
_____

> Incredible change happens in your life when you decided to take control of what you do have power over instead of craving control over what you don't.
> —Steve Maraboli

Success is waiting for you ...

S11

Come Here Fishy, Fishy, Fishy

Luke 5:6 (TPT)

Take 2: When they pulled up their nets, they were shocked to see a huge catch of fish, so much that their nets were ready to burst!

What stands out to me today is: where were all of those fish the night before? So, let's dive deep!

Do you believe in miracles? *What if* the fish heard the voice of Jesus and swam into the net? *What if* nature responds to His voice? Oh, wait, nature does. The trees clap their hands. I'm not crazy; go look it up for yourself.

I know this is a far-fetched idea for some. It depends on your background. When God created, He spoke it all into existence. However, there was a method in which He formed first, then He filled. He created the water, then the fish—in that order—so the water could sustain the fish. He created grass before the cow to sustain their hunger. You get the picture. He created your success for you to have it from the inside. I submit to you that your fish are awaiting the voice of the Creator. The question is: Is your spirit alert and listening? When Jesus calls the *fish* out of you, is there willingness of your free will to allow this? Get ready to haul in a bunch of fish from your nets. The voice of Jesus can be audible, but many times, it's what we feel or hear in our spirit.

Dip ...

So, what part of nature is waiting on your obedience, and when it hears Jesus' voice, will fill your nets?

_____
_____
_____
_____

Dive ---

What is the voice of Jesus directing you to do in the current season of your life? Peter listened to the voice of Jesus and was obedient, are you?

_____
_____
_____
_____

Drench ...

If your answer is yes, what is He telling you about your next season? If no, write a prayer right now. Ask Jesus to show you what the root of your *no* is. He will reveal it and even a solution on how to move forward.

_____
_____
_____
_____

Great spirits have always encountered violent opposition from mediocre minds.
—Albert Einstein

Success is waiting for you ...

S12

Profit

Luke 5:6 (TPT)

<u>Take 3:</u> *When they pulled up their nets, they were shocked to see a huge catch of fish, so much that their nets were ready to burst!*

Peter and his friends were gonna net a huge profit. First, they gotta figure out how to get sinking boats to shore, and they did. Next, they needed a strategy on how to sell all of those fish.

Peter's Daily Catch

Shop on the dock ~ Market price

Sushi kabobs ~ Add $2.00/lb.

Grilled on dock ~ Add $4.00/lb.

Some fish sold right from the wooden planks of the boat; others were scraped to remove the scales and wrapped. Still, others were grilled from the dock. Success can have a myriad of options that flow from one source. Many times, options create greater profit margins.

I've been in ministry for a long time, maybe too long. LOL! It is common to believe that profit is a dirty word, especially if we are believers. That's a lie! Jesus broke it down in Matthew 25:13-40 to three servants that profit is a *holy word*.

#1: Given five talents—Made five talents

    #100% Gain

#2: Given two talents—Made two talents

    #100% Gain

#3: Given one talent—Buried it in the ground. Yep, no kidding, he buried it.

    #Slothful

Jesus said to #1: "Whoa, bro, awesome job! You were entrusted with little; I will entrust you over much." #whoabro

Jesus said to #2: "Awesome, dude! You were entrusted with little; I will entrust you over much." #awesomedude

Jesus said to #3: "You wicked and slothful servant. I shouldn't have given you any at all. Give what you buried in the ground to Bro #1." I'm serious. I didn't make that up. This is the *lion* part of Jesus. #nodough

It's very interesting that Jesus used the term *talents*. It's not only money; it's the gifts He put inside of you. Gifts create different forms of profit. The gifts were put there for you to solve a problem, to make profit, to make a living, and to bless others. The list goes on.

Dip ...

In what arena is Jesus leading you to be successful and make a profit? Remember, profit isn't limited to money, but there isn't anything wrong with money. What does profit look like in your life? Can you wrap your brain around a myriad of options for more profit in your life?

_____
_____
_____
_____

Dive ---

Start a two-person *Think Tank* right now—you and Jesus: How is He telling you to create profit? Let the creative side of your brain create. 1 Corinthians 2:9 (NIV) says, *"What no eye has seen, what no ear has heard, and what no human mind has conceived"-the things God has prepared for those that love him-"* Take the next ten-15 minutes (set a timer), and write the results from your *Think Tank*.

_____
_____
_____
_____

Drench ...

Now, ask Jesus how He wants you to move forward. (BTW, if you have money in the jar buried in the yard, you better dig it up!)

_____
_____
_____
_____

A great merchant delivers both joy and profit. Then profit gets reinvested in more joy.
—Andy Dunn

Success is waiting for you ...

S13

Who's Gonna Help You?

Luke 5:7 (TPT)

They waved to their business partners in the other boat for help. They ended up completely filling both boats with fish until their boats began to sink!

One of the hardest things in life to do is to *cut people*. When I say that, people laugh, but I'm not talking about cutting with a knife; I'm talking about the tougher job of cutting them from your life. Who are you hanging with? Do they encourage you to do the right things? Are they *truth-tellers*? Do they share your zeal for Jesus? Do they push you toward your God goals? Do they take you away from Jesus?

Peter's friends still believed in Jesus, even though they were involved in the *night shift* failure. His friends were still there for him. I love to have friends who hang with me even after a failure. They knew Jesus was on the scene and didn't try to persuade Peter to leave. They were willing to help Peter fulfill his dream and move forward. Look, I don't like to fish, but I'm good with Jesus filling my net.

The word is clear when it talks about our Jesus friends. Ecclesiastes 4:12 (NIV) says, "Though one may be overpowered, two can defend themselves. A cord of three strands is not quickly broken." *The Message* sums it up like this: "By yourself, you're unprotected. With a friend you can face the worst. Can you round up a third? A three stranded rope isn't easily snapped." Peter + James + John = Three Stranded Cord! Such epic synergy comes from three.

Dip ...
So, the question is? Who is your support system? Who do you need to cut? How will you cut them while still showing the love of Jesus to them?

_____
_____
_____

Dive ---
Do you have a *soul sister* or a *soul bro*? That person who is an awesome friend who pushes you when it comes to your devotional time, prayer time, praise time. The friend is willing to clean the nets even through failure, will continue to help you, will tell you the truth, will laugh with you, will cry with you, and will tell you no.

_____
_____
_____

Drench ...
One last thought for the day: If you haven't met a Jesus friend who pushes and challenges you, write out a prayer below asking for your destiny path to cross theirs, so you can enjoy the fruit of the Jesus relationships. If you have a Jesus friend(s), list them below, and send them a quick text, Snapchat, or Facebook letting them know how thankful you are for them. Be specific and tell them why and how they have impacted your life.

_____
_____
_____

Of all possessions a friend is the most precious."
—Herodotus

Success is waiting for you ...

S14
J LOL

Luke 5:7 (TPT)

Take 2: They waved to their business partners in the other boat for help. They ended up completely filling both boats with fish until their boats began to sink!

I hope it was warm on this day. 'Cause when Peter's friends started to help him, the boats started to sink. That water would be refreshing on a warm day! We assume it's a bad day if our boats start to sink, but maybe our mindsets need a paradigm shift.

The heart of Jesus is kind and fun! Peter tells Jesus He's been fishing all night without catching anything. Jesus gives them a crazy solution, and when they listen to Him, their boats sink because of their success! I think Jesus was on the dock, *LOL*! I believe He was incredibly happy for them and amused by their amusement! Jesus' joy was contagious because the will of the Father and the promise of breaking out of the spiritual world into the physical world was evident in Peter's life. *His Kingdom come, His will be done.*

I wonder if He laughed when He said, "It is easier for a camel to go through the eye of a needle than for a rich person to enter the kingdom of God." That's like crazy, unbelievable, doesn't make sense funny!

And I love Proverbs 17:22 (TPT): *A joyful, cheerful heart brings healing to both body and soul. But the one whose heart is crushed struggles with sickness and depression.*

Wow, when it hits you in the face like that, why aren't you laughing? Many times, we take ourselves too seriously, especially with failures. It's time to lighten up and laugh. Heck, at least smile. Everyone around you will appreciate it!

Laughter is triggered in your brain. Then, a release of endorphins flow through your body, you relax, and the entire cerebral cortex is exercised. At that point, your blood sugar lowers, cortisol levels lower, you burn calories, relax your face muscles, and you feel better! The benefits of laughter are pretty amazing for our entire body.

The reason I know Jesus laughed, even though it doesn't line list it in the Bible is because of Proverbs 17:22: "A joyful, cheerful heart brings healing to both body and soul. (TPT) Jesus has a joyful and cheerful heart, and He desires that we catch His contagious heart and duplicate the results, creating awesome benefits!"

Dip ...
What makes you laugh?

_____
_____
_____
_____

Dive ---
How often do you laugh? Are you able to laugh at yourself?

_____
_____
_____
_____

Drench ...
When was the last time you laughed about a failure when you were trying to succeed? Imagine what Jesus' laugh sounds like. Journal your creative answer:

_____
_____
_____
_____

Today's seed is very different, and it's a tough seed to write about. Some people can't move past themselves in a serious way to allow the laughter of Jesus to motivate their hearts. Check out a Chonda Pierce video. She'll make you laugh until your belly hurts or water spills from areas you don't want it to. As your boat starts to *success sink*, Jesus is laughing as he watches from the dock. He's joyous, cheerful, and excited for you! Will you laugh with Him? Find what makes you laugh, and include it in your routine. Start today!

There is nothing in the world so irresistibly contagious as laughter and good humor.
—Charles Dickens, *A Christmas Carol*

Success is waiting for you ...

S15
Aahhh, the Aroma

Luke 5:7 (TPT)

<u>Take 3</u>: *"They waved to their business partners in the other boat for help. They ended up completely filling both boats with fish until their boats began to sink!"*

There would be that one seagull keeping an eye open on the Sea of Galilee, watching for the sign of a free meal. Once he spots it, the lookout bird would alert his friends with squawking, chirping, wailing, and flying in close, determined to get a midnight snack. The seagulls would caw to alert their feathered friends of free tilapia dinner, on a first-come, first-served basis.

Isn't it amazing how seagulls have exceptional eyesight, yet a marginal sense of smell? People are looking for your success, specifically how you can add value to them. Some will look, and others will smell when that unique smell of success saturates the air. With their spirit, they will smell and savor whatever you are willing to pour out. They need your gifts to grow to their next level of success in their life.

Your gifts were placed inside of you before the foundations of the earth and will satisfy others' hunger. Peter catching those fish allowed others to eat, physically and spiritually.

SEEDS OF SUCCESS

Dip ...
What gift/talent is inside of you that once released, will help others?

_____
_____
_____
_____

Dive ---
What problem drives you crazy that upon solving, you are fulfilled?

_____
_____
_____
_____

Drench ...
That, my friend, is what you are called to do in this lifetime. Offer a kingdom solution to that person/people group.

What is one thing you will commit to flow out of you in this season?

_____
_____
_____
_____

Little did I realize that my desire to add value to others would be the thing that added valued to me!
—John C. Maxwell

Success is waiting for you ...

S16
Balance the Fish

Luke 5:7 (TPT)

<u>Take 4</u>: *They waved to their business partners in the other boat for help. They ended up completely filling both boats with fish until their boats began to sink!*

Balancing success is challenging. How do you handle the new success with the old life, especially when the two seasons collide?

These changes result in decision. How will you move from the current season to the new season of success?

SEEDS OF SUCCESS

Dip ...
What does this type of success look like for you? What will you have to balance or give up to make room for this new-found success?

_____
_____
_____
_____

Dive ---
How will you maintain the water level in the boat without losing any fish? What is your plan when you need another boat to hold all of the fish?

_____
_____
_____
_____

Drench ...
If you have a balance ball/board, curb, etc., get on it, and balance yourself with some books, something breakable, etc. Your local gym may have a balance ball/board, etc. It's hard to balance our bodies, much less holding onto other stuff. What *stuff*, good or bad, do you need to take off of your plate so you can move into the new season and balance it correctly?

_____
_____
_____
_____

Happiness is not a matter of intensity but of balance, order, rhythm and harmony.
—Thomas Merton

Success is waiting for you ...

S17

Rhythm's Relation to Balance

Luke 5:7 (TPT)

<u>Take 5</u>: "They waved to their business partners in the other boat for help. They ended up completely filling both boats with fish until their boats began to sink!"

Many people have a *word* for a new year. At the beginning of 2019, my friend shared her word with me for the year, "trust." She asked me what my word was. Well, I didn't have one! She said to me, "You seem tired, and your life is so busy. Maybe your word should be "balance." I marveled that she could find my word so easily, yet I knew deep inside that I needed a different word. She saw my struggle and watched as tiredness crept into my life. Tired and frustrated, yet knowing there was more to come, how could I possibly balance more?

As I took a deeper look at myself, I noticed that in trying to balance my life, I hadn't considered the rhythms God had created for me to live by. I am an overachiever; I wear many hats all of the time, and that's part of who I am. I'm happier when I have more hats (within reason). I had allowed the *sound* of balance to take over my life and therefore, it knocked me out of rhythm. There is nothing worse than not being in rhythm for your life.

Balance is exhausting, trying to maintain the same % in every category in your life. Rhythm is being in sync with the creator of the universe, how He created you, what makes you tick, and how that naturally flows in and out of your life.

2018 held many transitions for me. I had been on that balance board that we talked about yesterday...I was exhausted and not happy. As soon as I got off of the balance board and starting flowing in my natural rhythms, joy starting flowing, the tiredness left, and fulfillment filled my soul. Be sure to be in balance when new seasons transition into your life, while remembering that rhythm supersedes balance for each individual person.

Jesus said it like this in *The Message* version of Matthew 11:28-30. *"Are you tired? Worn out? Burned out on religion? Come to me. Get away with me an you'll recover your life. I'll show you how to take a real rest. Walk with me and work with me-watch how I do it. Learn the unforced rhythms of grace. I won't lay anything heavy or ill-fitting on you. Keep company with me and you'll learn how to live freely and lightly."*

RHYTHM'S RELATION TO BALANCE

Dip ...
What are the natural rhythms in your life that God created just for you?

_____
_____
_____
_____

Dive ---
How do you move daily in your rhythms with Jesus?

_____
_____
_____
_____

Drench ...
What are tweaks that need to be made in your rhythm flow to move forward into success?

_____
_____
_____
_____

> As you get the rhythm, you discern how to win.
> —Miyamoto

Success is waiting for you ...

S18

Oh Snap, Jesus!

Luke 5:8 (TPT)

When Simon Peter saw this astonishing miracle, he knelt at Jesus' feet and begged him, "Go away from me, Master, for I am a sinful man!"

Depart from me …

Seriously, this is what Simon Peter said to Jesus? In Matthew 16:17, when Peter was the only disciple with supernatural understanding of who Jesus was, Jesus changed Peter's name from Simon to Peter, meaning Petros/Rock. Jesus then made a huge statement: Upon this rock, I will build my church, and the gates of Hades will not overcome it.

When Jesus changed Simon's name to Peter, He laid something down for Peter to pick up. He entered a new season. He was now *Petros/Rock*. This also occurred with Abraham as recapped in Romans 4:17 (NKJV), "(as it is written, "I have made you a father of many nations") in the presence of Him whom he believed-God, who gives life to the dead and calls those things which do not exist as though they did." Understand that you calling forth your new name has power … the power of death and life are in the tongue.

So, let's get this straight: Peter accepts the new name and goes forward. Then, success enters his life because of Jesus, but then He tells Jesus to depart. What's up with that?

2018 was a huge year for me, I became a Life Coach and author. I had to produce a video called "I Am An Author" and post it on Facebook as part of my assignment for my publishing company, Author Academy Elite. It was hard to put the video out there because I hadn't finished or published a book. It made me admit who Jesus said I was in the success season even though it hadn't manifested itself in the natural yet.

Dip ...
Who are you in this current success season of your life?

_____
_____
_____
_____

Dive ---
What simple selfie video do you need to produce and post so you can admit who you are in this success season? I double dog dare you to do it. Even if you don't post it, it is huge to admit the new season and call it forth in your life. What was your new name in the video?

_____
_____
_____
_____

Drench ...
What name are you calling forth that Jesus has already called you? Check out "You Say" by Lauren Daigle. What did you hear the voice of Jesus say in the song about you? Repeat it over and over, and make a post about it.

_____
_____
_____
_____

Success is waiting for you ...

S19
Self-Sabotage

Luke 5:8 (TPT)

<u>Take 2</u>: When Simon Peter saw this astonishing miracle, he knelt at Jesus' feet and begged him, "Go away from me, Master, for I am a sinful man!"

Ever prayed a stupid prayer? I have. Jesus, let me be your hands and feet. So spiritual, so holy—until He put that person in my life who needed me to *literally* be their hands and feet because they were blind.

Peter said a stupid prayer. *"Jesus depart from me."* Peter was in the very throws of success and asked Jesus to take it away. In other words, he self-sabotaged. Psychology today's definition of Self Sabotage: Behavior is said to be self-sabotaging when it creates problems and interferes with long-standing goals.[3]

Self-Sabotage is what we do when we can see, touch, smell, hear, and taste success. Its root is found in fear, leading back to the unknown change's success will bring to your life.

Peter was scared because his life was about to change, and He was losing control. So, He did what most success-seeking, next-level normal people do—He spouted off a stupid request. *"Go away from me, Master, for I am a sinful man!"*

He hadn't learned how to trust Jesus with his present, much less his future. This is how we self-sabotage from operating in new seasons and next-level living. It's time to protect ourselves against spiritual self-sabotage by applying Hebrews 4:12 (TPT), *For we have the living Word of God, which is full of energy, and it pierces more sharply than a two-edged sword. It will even penetrate to the very core of our being where soul and spirit, bone and marrow meet. It interprets and reveals the true thoughts and secret motives of our hearts.*

SELF-SABOTAGE

Dip ...

Have you self-sabotaged, consciously, or unconsciously? Let's set a strategy plan to fortify these areas in our life. What is the first clue that you are headed to self-sabotage?

_____
_____
_____
_____

Dive ---

Do you have an accountability partner set up when these clues present themselves to you? If yes, who and how do you contact them? If no, who will you ask to cover you in this area?

_____
_____
_____
_____

Drench ...

What verse in the Word of God will be your go-to verse when self-sabotage tries to operate in your life?

_____
_____
_____
_____

What lies behind us and what lies before us are tiny matters compared to what lies within us.
—Ralph Waldo Emerson

SEEDS OF SUCCESS

Self-sabotage is like a game of mental tug of war. It is the conscious mind versus the subconscious mind where the subconscious mind always eventually wins.
—Bo Bennett

Success is waiting for you …

S20

Jesus the Space Invader

Luke 5:8 (TPT)

<u>Take 3:</u> *When Simon Peter saw this astonishing miracle, he knelt at Jesus' feet and begged him, "Go away from me, Master, for I am a sinful man!"*

Ever met a space invader? You know, that person who just doesn't know when to zip it, when to get out of your face, when to not touch you? I have, and they drive me off of the deep end.

Peter and his friends experienced this. Where we hunker down in an overstuffed chair with a sweet tea moaning about how we failed, yet again. Success is so foreign to us that we collide with it and we don't know how to react to it. We must transition our minds to recognize success and capitalize on its sweetness.

Honey is sweet and sticky, like success! Can't you taste the sweetness when success invades your life? It takes a nano second to think of how we will *spend* success whether it's time, moolah, relationships, career, or something else.

Then, the realization of the stickiness—the twin to sweetness—is stirred up on the inside, and you start to cower at the fear of success. It's gonna change you, require more of you, and it's going to tax you in ways you have never been accountable for before (The IRS will tax you too, lol). Trying to figure out new schedules, transitions, new thought processes, new financial responsibility, and of course, how to expand and collapse time.

Yeah, success takes a lot!

As it tells us in Luke 12:48b (NKJV), "Whom much is given, from him much will be required"

JESUS THE SPACE INVADER

Dip ...

Jesus is a space invader. He invaded Peter's space, and He's working on yours right now. When your nets start to break, what new responsibilities do you foresee swimming into your life? What is your current priority list?

_____
_____
_____
_____

Dive ---

What will your new daily priority schedule look like? Think big. When your nets are breaking and life has changed, how will you maintain that priority list?

_____
_____
_____
_____

Drench ...

What areas of success can you be entrusted with? What areas of success are a struggle for you to be entrusted with? Who is your support system to help you overcome in the struggle areas? Take time to pray now for those struggle areas, and thank Him for the strong areas.

_____
_____
_____
_____

In any given moment we have two options: to step forward into growth or to step back into safety.
—Abraham Maslow

Success is waiting for you ...

S21

Unworthy

Luke 5:8 (TPT)

<u>Take 4</u>: *When Simon Peter saw this astonishing miracle, he knelt at Jesus' feet and begged him, "Go away from me, Master, for I am a sinful man!"*

Ever felt unworthy? I spent half of my life not feeling worthy of anything. Self-worth can't be taught; it has to be caught directly from the heart of God the Father. Peter had to *catch* self-worth to understand that he had been placed on this earth for that such time and had an important assignment.

Legalism spoke to Peter that day, and he listened. He felt unworthy to be in the presence of Jesus. Life throws us that curveball when we succeed. It's that recognizable voice that you're not good enough. Shut the front door! Jesus died and rose again for our sins and our unworthiness. When God looks at us, He sees His Son, perfection through our imperfection. We're not worthy of ourselves, but because of the blood of Jesus, God sees us as worthy.

Or could it have been Peter was being lazy and didn't want to accept the responsibility of the success? What would Jesus expect Peter to do now?

SEEDS OF SUCCESS

Dip ...
What success have you experienced that you ask Jesus to take away or depart from you?

_____
_____
_____

Dive ---
I challenge you today to accept the success Jesus has brought you. If the feelings of unworthiness are trying to take you down, tell them directly: "Unworthy, you have no right or reign in my life," I am a child of God. So, leave, hit the road, Jack. Bye, Felicia!

_____
_____
_____

Drench ...
Check out this video to go deeper today: No Longer Slaves— Johnathon & Melissa Hesler

https://m.youtube.com/watchv=XxkNj5hcy5E

_____
_____
_____

Success is waiting for you ...

S22

Ignored from the Throne Room

Luke 5:8 (TPT)

Take 5: When Simon Peter saw this astonishing miracle, he knelt at Jesus' feet and begged him, "Go away from me, Master, for I am a sinful man!"

Perception in our lives is huge. Many times, what we perceive as Jesus ignoring us is grace from the throne room. Think about it. Jesus gave Peter so many fish that the nets started to sink but they caught nothing alone. When this happened, Peter asked Jesus to leave him because he was a sinful man. Ya think?

Grace is defined as getting what you don't deserve. Peter *deserved* for Jesus to leave; it's what He asks him to do—depart from me. The lamb side of Jesus showed!

Perception tells us that Jesus ignored Peter's request, when, in actuality, Jesus was giving Peter grace. The depth of Jesus' love for Peter came through loud and louder. I love you too much to leave you, Peter. Jesus then answers from the throne room, "Peter, do not yield to your fear." It was the Lion voice of Jesus, commanding, yet loving. His love surpasses all *stupid* prayers. His grace always triumphs, disguised as love.

SEEDS OF SUCCESS

Dip ...
What is the most current perception that you have been asking Jesus for? Do you feel you are being ignored by Jesus or do you feel His grace? What is He telling you not be afraid of?

_____
_____
_____
_____

Dive ---
Listen closely to His voice. There will be obvious clues as to what your next season entails. So, when He speaks "don't be afraid of _____," journal what the Spirit of Jesus is sharing with your spirit:

_____
_____
_____
_____

Drench ...
How is His grace triumphing over your perceptions, disguised as love?

_____
_____
_____
_____

The eye sees only what the mind is prepared to comprehend.
—Henri Bergson

Success is waiting for you ...

S23
Comfort = Failure

Luke 5:8 (TPT)

<u>Take 6:</u> *When Simon Peter saw this astonishing miracle, he knelt at Jesus' feet and begged him, "Go away from me, Master, for I am a sinful man!"*

Comfort is that place where you land and don't want to leave. Comfort loves company, especially when comfort = failure.

Self-pity is easy to wallow in when you fail. Everybody knows what failure feels like. Many try to one up their misery partner with comparing notes of why their failure was worse.

Jesus' comfort zone was confronted in the Garden of Gethsemane. He grew accustomed to life as He knew it, and all of a sudden, it was time to go to the cross. He found himself in the dirt, on His knees, crying out to Daddy God. With drops of bloody sweat running down his forehead into his eyes, He asked His father, God: "If you can take this cup from me, take it. If not, I'll do it." I wonder if Jesus felt the fear of success (He was 100% man and 100% God). What would death taste like? What would it feel like? What would the natural process of death be like? Would it all be worth it? Would His Daddy turn His eyes back on Jesus when the sin infiltrated his very being? Jesus was pure, perfect, and holy, yet He became all of our sin.

Comfort was stripped, and to add insult to injury, He experienced the crushing pressure of moving forward into His new season of success. His new season was that of total freedom, healing, and legalism abolished for us. And He's moving back to His old stomping grounds.

COMFORT = FAILURE

Dip ...
How is Jesus confronting your comfort zone? Are you crying out to Daddy God asking Him to take this cup from you?

_____
_____
_____
_____

Dive ---
If He takes the cup away, how will you feel and respond? If God decides, as a loving Father, to not take the cup from you, how will you respond to this?

_____
_____
_____
_____

Drench ...
Are you at the place to say, "Not my will, but yours be done?" In other words, I'll move out of my comfort zone. I'll enter the new season of catching a different type of fish, having to go deep, and having to offer more energy to clean my nets once again. Are you at that place? Journal where you are with it all.

_____
_____
_____
_____

> The best things in life are often waiting for you
> at the exit ramp of your comfort zone.
> —Karen Salmansohn

Success is waiting for you ...

S24

Next Level

Luke 5:8 (TPT)

Take 7: When Simon Peter saw this astonishing miracle, he knelt at Jesus' feet and begged him, "Go away from me, Master, for I am a sinful man!"

Your next level is so large you must change your container to hold the blessings. Jesus said it this way: *"And no one puts new wine into old wineskins."* He was saying, you can't put the next level blessing into the current season container. To move forward, you must create an honorable, fresh container for God to fill with His new wine. It's not about performance.

Peter had to switch out his failure container to one of success to hold that precious, fresh wine! Peter's negative mindset couldn't steward the changes of being a successful fisherman. Total fear kept the negative mindset working and blocked positivity. He then reverted to "I am a sinful man." Seriously? He played *the feel sorry for me card* with Jesus of all people. How about you? Have you brought out that deck of cards to shuffle and dealt them to Jesus? Newsflash: Jesus doesn't play that game. He only plays UNO™. He's only asking for a new container, and then He will bless your socks off with new wine. But like Peter, it will require a new container from you.

SEEDS OF SUCCESS

Dip ...
What is your "negative mindset"?

_____
_____
_____
_____

Dive ---
What area of your life needs to have a "new container" to hold the next move of Jesus?

_____
_____
_____
_____

Drench ...
What has Jesus shared with you about your next level of life?

_____
_____
_____
_____

You are a container with the ability to increase your capacity. Doing so will take you to the next level.
—Donette W. Spence

Success is waiting for you ...

S25
Awestruck

Luke 5:9–10 (TPT)

Simon Peter and the other fishermen—including his fishing partners, Jacob and John, the sons of Zebedee-were awestruck over the miracle catch of fish. Jesus answered, "Do not yield to your fear, Simon Peter. From now on you will catch men for salvation!"

Awestruck: To be full of complete wonder, a feeling of complete amazement.

The fishermen understood what it was like to be *awestruck*. They had witnessed a miracle of the most high Jesus! It was the aroma, touch, and energy infusion of a miracle.

It is our responsibility to recognize success was planted in us. To breathe and have provision for every day is a miracle, and to have success planted in us before the foundations of the earth is a miracle.

We were made for success and to utilize our gifts to solve problems for others. Your gifts aren't for you; that's a consumer mindset. The Kingdom principle is for us. It is better to give than to receive.

What problem do you see in the world that your gifts will solve? You may be the only person on planet earth with the ability to pour into that one person and solve the issue. Wow! That's a miracle!

We normally think awestruck refers to a miracle in front of our eyes. But what about the day you were created? That is an awestruck moment!

The big thing now is your heart. Will you make a commitment to keep your heart pure when you see the miracles? A miracle can be any type of breakthrough: emotional, spiritual, financial, relational, mental—the sky is the limit! For those miracles to manifest, the power of Jesus will be released through your gifts. Awestruck is seeing the miracle and giving Jesus the credit.

Dip ...

What gifts were placed in you before the foundations of the earth? How will you utilize just one of those gifts during and directly after this 31-day challenge?

_____
_____
_____
_____

Dive ---

What specific solution to what specific problem was planted in you? What miracles could you see from utilizing the one thing? Be real here. Dream big, and dive into the unknown. It's not pride; it's a reality.

_____
_____
_____
_____

Drench ...

Will you keep your heart pure to give the glory to Jesus? Will you have a heart accountability partner or heart friend you can talk to if your heart starts to beat in a different direction? The person(s) you can be transparent with and they will still love you?

_____
_____
_____
_____

Keep your head and your heart going in the right direction and you will not have to worry about your feet.
—Dr. Myles Monroe

Pride is pleasure arising from man's thinking
too highly of himself.
—Baruch Spinoza

Success is waiting for you …

S26

Fear Stinks

Luke 5:9–10 (TPT)

Take 2: Simon Peter and the other fishermen—including his fishing partners, Jacob and John, the sons of Zebedee-were awestruck over the miracle catch of fish. Jesus answered, "Do not yield to your fear, Simon Peter. From now on you will catch men for salvation!"

I John 4:18 (KJV) tells us, "But perfect love casteth out fear." When we are scared, our bodies produce a hormone called adrenaline. Adrenaline puts off a scent that attracts predators. Our dog, Lexi, has always been adventurous. She loves the outdoors and wants to check out anything in *her* yard and street. She loves to chase the squirrels although she never seems to catch one. However, she met her match one night in our yard. We had major issues with skunks in our neighborhood, and they decided to become tenants under the storage building in our yard. Free rent! Yep, you see where this is going, and it stinks!

Lexi's nose was so interested in the *smell* from outside that she barked insistently until we let her out. I thought she only needed to water the yard and was being a diva! Well, two minutes later, she was back on the porch with her tail tucked and those big brown eyes looking at us with shame. Yes, she had been skunked and wanted back in the house. I opened the door and shut it super-fast. She'd attracted the smell of the skunk so much it permeated her very being and caused her shame.

Lexi still goes crazy when she smells a skunk and wants to check it out. She's been skunked three times now, but who's counting?

We all experience fear, and that's going to happen. However, what we do with the fear is the important piece. When we allow fear to attach itself to us, it creates a smell that attracts the predators of shame, rejection, and failure, and it stinks!

Snakes sense fear, dogs know when we're scared of them, elephants can sniff it out, and so can bees. Yes, we *bark* at Jesus because *we want to be let out* to be *skunked* once again. The only way to get rid of that smell is to allow God's perfect love to cast the fear out.

FEAR STINKS

Dip ...
What is the current area of fear in your life?

_____
_____
_____
_____

Dive ---
What would it look like if you were to triumph over that fear?
(Be specific)

_____
_____
_____
_____

Drench ...
What one step will you take today to conquer the fear you listed?

_____
_____
_____
_____

> I learned that courage was not the absence of fear, but the triumph over it. The brave man is not he who does not feel afraid, but he who conquers that fear.
> —Nelson Mandela

Success is waiting for you ...

S27
From Now On

Luke 5:10 (TPT)

Take 3: "Jesus answered, "Do not yield to your fear, Simon Peter. From now on you will catch men for salvation!"

These men's career paths were about to change in a life altering way. Holy smokes, their *catch category* would change from slippery when wet to *be careful with my heart*. It was scary, and they certainly didn't have a degree or training in catching men.

Your life path will take a radical trajectory change as you move into success. Your *from now on* will create waves of change as your new *fish* jump out of the water! Removing the hook from the mouth of a fish is totally different than unhooking a human heart of unbelief.

My *from now on* is to be positive. As much as I have been around negativity for the majority of my life, I have managed to be super positive. However, if I evaluate each day, I can pinpoint where and when I'm not positive. We need to be accountable to be effective.

John 8:32 tells us the truth will set us free. It's painful but necessary. Pain is the process to promotion. I encourage you to be truthful with yourself. Now is super important in your life as it will propel you into the future.

SEEDS OF SUCCESS

Dip ...
So, what is your *from now on*?

_____
_____
_____
_____

Dive ---
How will you implement your *from now on*?

_____
_____
_____
_____

Drench ...
What does your *from now on* look like? Be detailed, dream, and proclaim!

_____
_____
_____
_____

It's time to start living the life you've imagined
—Henry James

Success is waiting for you ...

S28
Intimate Vulnerability Vessel

Luke 5:10–11 (TPT)

<u>Take 4</u>: *Jesus answered, "Do not yield to your fear, Simon Peter. From now on you will catch men for salvation!" After pulling their boats to the shore, they left everything behind and followed Jesus.*

Peter's boat was the place that housed his identity and where he felt irritation and failure. Identity + Irritation = Exasperation and Esteem crisis. Jesus was aware of the current Peter equation and still stood boldly in Peter's boat with a request. Leave your current life of fishing in exchange for a life of intimacy and belonging with Jesus.

Intimacy is a tough decision. It wasn't popular then, and it's certainly not popular in today's society. Intimacy creates an atmosphere of vulnerability and requires commitment. Vulnerable: capable of being physically or emotionally wounded. No wonder we don't want to be intimate; it requires the vulnerability of opening up the soul and allows others to see the real and raw you. Yikes!

Jesus knows what intimacy is. He is one with the Father and the Holy Spirit. The three in one modeled intimacy during the creation process. Each worked through their own personality, with unity and the same end goal in mind, exposing everything to the other two. Jesus also opened himself up to the 12 disciples. He allowed them to see his hurt, pain, disappointments, expectations, His anger, and His soul.

Ever shared an idea with someone and they totally rejected it or laughed at it? Yep, that's intellectual intimacy 101. It hurts because you opened yourself and became vulnerable. The boat had been a place of disappointment. Jesus turns the current atmosphere of Peter's boat into a vessel of intimacy. Peter has a decision to make, and so do you. Jesus is asking for your intimacy today.

How? Lean in to Jesus. Talk to him, and listen to what He says to you and what He impresses on your heart. Completely open your heart to Him, exposing the depth of who you are, and let Him know you desire intimacy with Him.

He will impart peace to you, giving you hope for your destiny. Yes, you will be vulnerable to Jesus, but He will always honor that vulnerability with His love, which brings intimacy.

Peter left his fishing career and allowed Jesus to change the failing atmosphere of his boat to a vessel of intimacy.

INTIMATE VULNERABILITY VESSEL

Dip ...
What does intimacy with Jesus look like to you?

_____
_____
_____
_____

Dive ---
Journal anything that hinders you from experiencing intimacy with Jesus. Then turn those things over to Him to open up 100% intimacy with Him.

_____
_____
_____
_____

Drench ...
Take some time now to spend intimate time with Jesus. You will be filled up, experience joy and understand peace that passes all understanding. Journal this precious time with Him:

_____
_____
_____
_____

Royalty is my identity. Servanthood is my assignment.
Intimacy with God is my life source.
—Bill Johnson

Success is waiting for you ...

S29
Opening & Closing Seasons

Luke 5:10–11 (TPT)

Take 5: Jesus answered, *"Do not yield to your fear, Simon Peter. From now on you will catch men for salvation!" After pulling their boats to the shore, they left everything behind and followed Jesus."*

Okay, so life on this planet ebbs and flows in seasons. I don't mean the four seasons; I mean the seasons of your soul. Parker J. Palmer writes about "the turning of the seasons" in *Let Your Life Speak*. Many of us have experienced the turning of our personal soul seasons.[4]

There are the fresh, exciting seasons, and the seasons we feel will never end. Jesus, without reservation or apology, asked Peter to close one season and open the next without any warning. There was no time for goodbyes, no time to plan, no time to *get his life in order*. Peter did as he was asked but with some reservation, of course. (Remember the stupid prayer?)

There are many opinions when the winds of opening or closing seasons starts to blow.

Dip ...

What season change is Jesus alerting you to right now, maybe without notice? Who will be excited for you to close/open this new season?

_____
_____
_____

Dive ---

Who will not be happy and even give you a hard time about closing one season to open another? Who would you rather make happy, the people for or against the whole season change leaving idea? Or Jesus? Okay, it was a low blow.
What's your answer?

_____
_____
_____

Drench ...

What is the old season and new season Jesus is asking you to change? Realistically, will you leave the old season and embark on the new?

_____
_____
_____

OPENING & CLOSING SEASONS

Prayer: Father, I know I have self-control, but I need some help down here. I'm asking for courage to walk away from the old season and move into the new one. I'll operate in whatever season you have for me, whether it's a layover or a destination stop. I'll get out and then get in. I'm looking forward to seeing more of what You have for me to grow Your kingdom.

You can't reach your potential by remaining in a past season. Your breakthrough is coming. Strongholds are breaking.
Get Ready!
—Germany Kent

Success is waiting for you ...

S30

The Complexity of Success

Luke 5:10–11 (TPT)

Take 6: Jesus answered, "Do not yield to your fear, Simon Peter. From now on you will catch men for salvation!" After pulling their boats to the shore, they left everything behind and followed Jesus."

Success is much more complex than failure. Failure means that you go back to the drawing board and rehash what didn't work and try to figure out what did. On the other hand, success makes you think with the creative side of your brain into the great unknown that only the Holy Spirit knows.

Questions buzz around in your head like a bumblebee. *How can I manage all of the fish? Who's gonna clean them? Who's gonna filet them? Who's gonna package them? How will I market them?*

I have to keep up with my new economy and be sure to hear the voice of God so I bless others. Oh, yeah, and don't forget to pay the taxes. Shew! That is hard stuff to work through.

How will you allocate your time so it serves you to be the most productive? How will you account for the new streams of income? Will you still spend time With God even though you've made it to this next level? How will you manage social media now that everyone knows about your success?

The complexity of success is huge, but super exciting!

Dip ...
You made it. You succeeded. How has your mindset about success changed?

_____
_____
_____
_____

Dive ---
Jesus said to Peter, "Don't be afraid, from now on you will fish for people." What are your old fish, and what are you fishing for now?

_____
_____
_____
_____

Drench ...
Social media is a huge tool in today's world. How will you use it effectively for your success without allowing pride to enter in?

_____
_____
_____
_____

Success means your options multiply. Size increases complexity, and complexity can confuse vision.
—Andy Stanley

Success is waiting for you ...

S31
Wildest Imagination Exceeded

Ephesians 3:20 (TPT)

Never doubt God's mighty power to work in you and accomplish all this. He will achieve infinitely more than your greatest request, your most unbelievable dream, and exceed your wildest imagination! He will outdo them all, for his miraculous power constantly energizes you.

You did it! Today is 31 days of soul-searching hard work! I know you laughed, cried, sweat, and threatened to quit, and I'm so proud of you. You made it!

Congratulations!!!!!!

SEEDS OF SUCCESS

Dip: ...
In detail, define the definition of success in your life and how it feels with your current success:

_____
_____
_____
_____

Dive ---
Today, you have planted 31 seeds into your life. What did you plant, and what are your expectations for your wildest imagination to be exceeded?

_____
_____
_____
_____

Drench ...
What will you do with your wildest imagination exceeded?

_____
_____
_____
_____

Note to self: The seeds of unimaginable success are within me.
—Katrina McGhee

Success is waiting for you ...

One Last Deep Drench Dive ...---...

You planted 31 seeds into your destiny. You also planted 31 days of the Word of God into the very essence of your being. From the 31 seeds, what is your #1 takeaway as a child of God? The truth that you will never let go of, the thing that changed the inside of you as a person? Dive deep; it will be worth it!

> There is no passion to be found playing small - in settling for a life that is less than the one you are capable of living.
> —Nelson Mandela

You found success—Congrats!

Endnotes

1. Admin. "The Myth of Multitasking." Psychology Smart, March 17, 2019. http://www.psychologysmart.com/2019/02/13/the-myth-of-multitasking/.

2. MacKay, By: Jory. "Productivity in 2017: What We Learned from Analyzing 225 Million Hours - RescueTime," March 20, 2018. https://blog.rescuetime.com/225-million-hours-productivity/.

3. "Self-Sabotage." Psychology Today. Sussex Publishers. Accessed August 30, 2020. https://www.psychologytoday.com/us/basics/self-sabotage.

4. Palmer, Parker J. "There Is a Season." Essay. In *Let Your Life Speak: Listening for the Voice of Vocation*, 95–109. San Francisco, ca: Jossey-Bass, 2000.

About the Author

Donette Spence is a passionate life coach, speaker, mentor and lead pastor who helps individuals discover their empowered life. She will pierce your heart with her *Real & Raw*, yet humorous style. Adding value to your life as *your* #1 encourager, she will show you how to walk in total freedom. It makes her heart happy to experience the depth of Jesus with you. She will challenge and empower you to experience every desire that God placed in your heart.

Donette and *The Love of her Life*, Randy, have enjoyed 34 fun years of marriage in Salem, VA and Dallas, TX. Lots of Crazy, Lots of Loud & Bunches of Love describe her amazing family: Daughters who double as friends, Kristen & Brittany; Super fun Son-in-Law, Maxwell; Gorgeous, fun and active Grandkids, Baxter & Eliza; her salt & pepper dog, Lexi; and chocolate brown Granddog, Cola. Y'all make life fun and adventurous!

donettespence.com, realandraw.withdonette@gmail.com

www.ingramcontent.com/pod-product-compliance
Lightning Source LLC
LaVergne TN
LVHW011726060526
838200LV00051B/3043